Searchlight
BOOKS™

Fear Fest

Eerie

ESP

Tracy Nelson Maurer

Lerner Publications ◆ Minneapolis

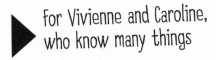

For Vivienne and Caroline,
who know many things

3 1969 02564 6315

Lerner Publications Company
A division of Lerner Publishing Group, Inc.
241 First Avenue North
Minneapolis, MN 55401 USA

For reading levels and more information, look up this title
at www.lernerbooks.com.

Library of Congress Cataloging-in-Publication Data

The Cataloging-in-Publication Data for *Eerie ESP* is on file at the Library
of Congress.
ISBN 978-1-5124-3404-0 (lib. bdg.)
ISBN 978-1-5124-5604-2 (pbk.)
ISBN 978-1-5124-5075-0 (EB pdf)

Manufactured in the United States of America
1-42040-23910-3/10/2017

Contents

Chapter 1

WHAT IS ESP?

Let's say your phone rings at seven on a Saturday morning, a time when most of your family and friends are still asleep. You instantly know it's your cousin calling. You don't know why you know. You just know. Sure enough, when you answer the phone, it's your cousin! Do you have ESP (extrasensory perception)?

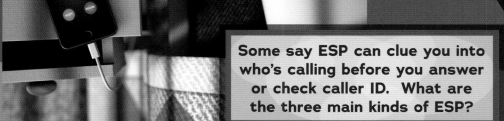

Some say ESP can clue you into who's calling before you answer or check caller ID. What are the three main kinds of ESP?

Most people use their five senses to understand the world: sight, sound, taste, touch, and smell. But what if the mind can "know" things without using those five senses? Some people believe it can! This ability to know without relying on the senses is what ESP is all about.

ESP refers to three main kinds of mental abilities beyond what science can explain:

- sensing the future, called precognition
- sensing what someone else is thinking, called telepathy
- sensing information about a place or event with no prior knowledge of it, called clairvoyance

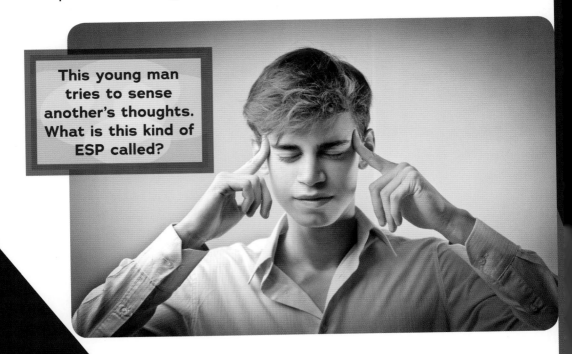

This young man tries to sense another's thoughts. What is this kind of ESP called?

Precognition

Many people who claim to experience precognition see the future in their dreams. Some researchers believe this is because the mind is most open to ESP when the body is resting. Others say the phenomenon of precognition is really just coincidence. They point out that there is no concrete proof ESP is real.

SOME BELIEVE OUR ESP ABILITIES ARE STRONGEST WHEN WE'RE ASLEEP.

Fact or Fiction?

Was the *Titanic*'s sinking really foretold in a novel fourteen years earlier?

It's uncertain. Read the facts and decide for yourself.

In 1898, author Morgan Robertson wrote a story about a luxury ocean liner named *Titan* that was thought to be unsinkable. This fictional ship sailed in early April across the Atlantic and struck an iceberg off the coast of Newfoundland. Thousands of passengers died because the ship did not have enough lifeboats. Sound familiar?

The *Titanic (above)* sank in much the same way that Robertson described in the story about the *Titan*.

Would you like to use telepathy to read your best friend's mind?

Telepathy

The word *telepathy* comes from the ancient Greek words *tele*, meaning "distant," and *pathos*, meaning "feeling." People may claim they receive information about a person out of nowhere. Perhaps you *just know* when your friend buys new earbuds, even though you had no idea before it happens.

Telepathy is a form of mind reading too. Knowing what others are thinking could be helpful. Friends would know where to meet one another without saying a word. Restaurant servers wouldn't have to ask for your order. But there's also a dark side to telepathy. Would you *really* want another person knowing your every thought?

Clairvoyance

Clairvoyance has been studied as a way to help police investigators, scientists, and government agencies. In 1973, artist Ingo Swann tried to see Jupiter with only his mind in a US government experiment. During his "remote viewing," he reported seeing a ring around the planet and described what that ring looked like. Scientists scoffed at first. But years later, space missions confirmed that the ring really did exist!

Swann's description of the planet Jupiter was eerily accurate!

The US government also hired at least sixteen psychics to practice remote viewing between 1970 and the mid-1990s in California. In one of the remote-viewing sessions, a US psychic spy discovered a previously unknown Russian military building used for missile construction in Siberia. Still, the US government was not convinced ESP was a valuable tool. The government closed the program.

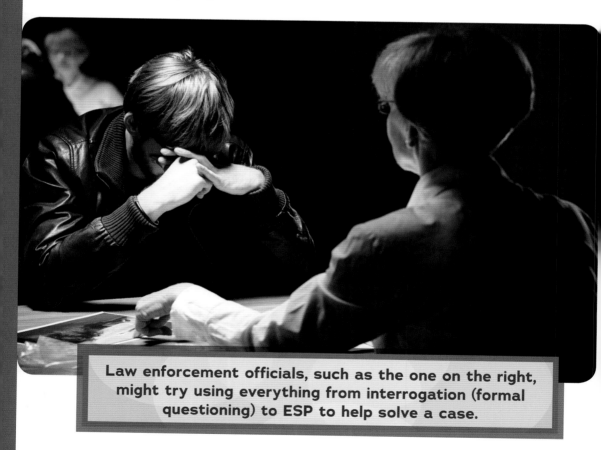

Law enforcement officials, such as the one on the right, might try using everything from interrogation (formal questioning) to ESP to help solve a case.

The US government isn't the only group that's experimented with remote viewing. After terrorists attacked New York City's twin towers in the World Trade Center complex in 2001, the British Ministry of Defence recruited psychics to use remote viewing to find Osama bin Laden, the man behind the attacks. The program closed before he was eventually found. Could the psychics have helped to find bin Laden? Not everyone agrees.

New York City's twin towers were destroyed in the 2001 terrorist attacks. A building called One World Trade Center stands near where the towers were.

Chapter 2

WHAT'S THE HISTORY OF ESP?

No one knows how long ago people began claiming to have ESP. Evidence suggests people have believed in paranormal powers for thousands of years. At the Temple of Apollo at Delphi in Greece, a woman called the Pythia would provide answers she claimed came from the Greek god Apollo. Priests would then explain the answers.

This is the Temple of Apollo at Delphi. Who was Apollo?

Nostradamus and His Prophecies

By the sixteenth century, psychics could be burned at the stake in Europe. People didn't trust those who claimed to have psychic abilities. A French psychic named Nostradamus even purposely kept his prophecies vague so he couldn't be labeled a psychic. He didn't want to risk being killed.

Nostradamus *(left)* wrote a book of prophecies in 1555. Some believe his book foretold events such as the death of King Louis XVI of France and the French Revolution (1789–1799).

Fact or Fiction?

ESP inspired a new art movement in the twentieth century.

It's a fact!

In the early twentieth century, Hélène Smith gained fame as a psychic medium (someone who communicates with faraway beings or the dead) when she claimed she could communicate with Martians. She would fall into a trance, and a spirit would guide her on mental trips to Mars. She would then produce writing in the Martian language and paintings of Mars. Smith's writing and paintings helped to launch surrealism, an art form that was also dreamlike and otherworldly.

Salvador Dalí may be the most famous surrealist painter. He painted the picture on the left.

ESP: Trendy in the Nineteenth Century

ESP and the paranormal became fashionable in the late nineteenth and early twentieth centuries. Many psychic mediums claimed an ability to communicate with the dead. Mary Todd Lincoln, the widow of President Abraham Lincoln, believed in the power of mediums, and she often attended séances.

Mary Todd Lincoln was a paranormal believer!

Many fake mediums were exposed in the nineteenth century. In response to the hoaxes, the Society for Psychical Research was founded in England in 1882. This group aimed to learn how ESP worked and what caused it. The group even came up with tests and mathematical formulas to identify the odds of experiencing an ESP event. People in the nineteenth century really wanted to get to the bottom of whether ESP is real or not—just as we do today!

THIS DOOR LED TO THE SOCIETY FOR PSYCHICAL RESEARCH. WOULD YOU LIKE TO GO INSIDE?

Chapter 3

WHO MIGHT HAVE ESP?

ESP may be a kind of rare sixth sense that only a few people have—or maybe it's a mental power that everyone has, but most people just don't know how to unlock it. The human mind is complex. Is it possible that humans could tap into far more of their brainpower with training or technology? And if we could, should we?

The human brain can do some amazing things, so not everyone believes only certain people have the gift of ESP. What's another theory?

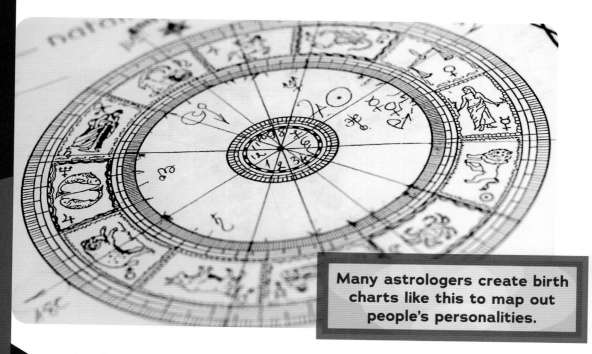

Many astrologers create birth charts like this to map out people's personalities.

No Psychic License Needed

No rules, exams, or licenses exist about who can have psychic abilities. Psychics come from all around the world and use a variety of methods to access their ESP. Some have claimed to develop their psychic abilities after brain injuries or trauma. Others practice reading palms, supposedly telling the future using the hand's creases.

In many cultures, astrologers are believed to have special powers to see the future. They read the positions of the planets when a person is born and draw a birth chart that shows the planets in the twelve signs of the zodiac.

Can Children Have ESP?

In the 1980s, a British TV show featured a man named Uri Geller supposedly bending spoons with his mind. Many kids soon claimed to be able to do the same thing. Paranormal researchers wondered if anyone of any age could have telekinesis abilities—a type of ESP in which a person sends mental messages to move objects.

Researchers invited kids who said they could bend spoons to demonstrate their powers in experiments. The children really did bend spoons! However, researchers soon figured out how they did it. They watched the kids from behind hidden windows. The kids simply used distractions and subtle hand movements while they forcefully bent the spoons. It was all a hoax.

Geller demonstrates spoon bending in 2008.

Fact or Fiction?

You can learn to bend spoons with your mind.

Well . . . not exactly. But you can make it look as if you can!

Here's what you do: Find a cheap, thin spoon. Hold the spoon between your thumb and index finger at the topmost part of the handle where the metal is thinnest. Distract your audience as magicians do, by telling a story or waving your empty hand. At the same time, rub the spoon with your fingers as fast as you can. Keep the audience from looking at your fingers. Rubbing the spoon creates friction that heats the metal and eventually softens it. Ta-da! You can bend it with your amazing mental abilities!

Bending spoons is a trick anyone can learn. Would you like to try it?

Animals with ESP

Even animals have been thought to have ESP. When tsunamis smashed into Thailand, India, and other Asian countries in 2004, most of the animals in the region had fled to higher ground before the first wave destroyed homes and drowned people. Animals seem to have an extraordinary sense of when disaster is about to hit.

Maybe animals just have a naturally keen sensitivity to changes in the environment that alerts them to danger. Or maybe the animals really did have ESP. No one has been able to give a concrete explanation for the animals' behavior on that day in 2004.

This photo shows destruction in Thailand after the 2004 tsunami. Fewer animals than expected lost their lives in the disaster.

Chapter 4

CAN WE EVER FIND THE TRUTH?

People have been studying ESP for decades. Joseph Banks Rhine researched telepathy and telekinesis in the 1920s. He created the term *ESP* and helped launch the study of paranormal events, called parapsychology. He and his wife, Louisa, wanted to show evidence of ESP based on scientific methods. That meant developing tests that other scientists could repeat to achieve the same results.

Joseph Banks Rhine and Louisa Rhine studied the paranormal. What is the study of paranormal events called?

One of Rhine's associates, Dr. Karl Zener, created five cards for ESP research in the 1930s. Each card has one of five symbols: a circle, a square, a cross, a star, or three wavy lines. A deck has twenty-five cards.

In some experiments, researchers asked people to guess the order of the cards in a shuffled deck. In others, researchers watched as one person looked at a card and tried to send a thought message about it to another person. That person tried to guess which card was in the thought message. Everyone has a one in five chance of correctly guessing the symbol on the card. If a person guesses correctly more times than one in five, then, according to Zener, that person may have ESP.

Zener cards like these are a tool for studying ESP.

Fact or Fiction?

You could get a job working with ESP someday.

It's a fact!

Parapsychologists around the world still study ESP. These scientists want to learn more about the human mind and its abilities. Some of their findings have revealed important information about how humans can be deceived by hoaxes.

You could work at a university, creating ways to test for ESP that use scientific methods. Or maybe you'll study remote viewing or telekinesis for a government or its spies. And if you have ESP, maybe you already know how you'll apply your skills!

Some people make a career out of studying ESP.

James Randi *(above)* loves magic but hates scams! He digs into whether ESP claims are true or false.

Magical Skeptics

Many professional magicians have been skeptical of ESP for decades. Magician James Randi is a well-known ESP skeptic. Randi works with parapsychologists to help identify fake claims. His skills at creating illusions onstage have helped to unlock some of the frauds' techniques. After all, who knows a fake better than a faker?

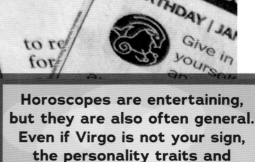

Horoscope

HOROS

WEEKLY FORECAST*

UTURE HOLDS AT

to re
for

BIRTHDAY | JA

Give in
yoursel

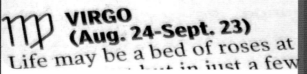

♍ **VIRGO**
(Aug. 24–Sept. 23)
Life may be a bed of roses at
but in just a few

> Horoscopes are entertaining, but they are also often general. Even if Virgo is not your sign, the personality traits and predictions for this sign might still be a good match for you.

Can You Tell a Hoax?

Sometimes it's just plain fun to believe that people have special mental powers. Many popular books and movies have featured characters with ESP. But they are fiction. How can you tell if a real-life story of ESP is true?

Look for too many remarkable coincidences, predictions that never came true, or wishful thinking on the part of the storyteller. Some who claim to be psychics use general words and phrases that could apply to anyone. Try reading your horoscope from a different zodiac symbol, for example. You'll probably find that much of the horoscope could fit you.

Even when skeptics point out things that are clearly *not* ESP, many people still want to prove ESP is possible. In the twenty-first century, ESP research has continued at more than a hundred universities and institutions in the United States and thirty other countries. A great deal of data exists about paranormal events. Science knows more than ever about the power of the human brain. Perhaps a lot remains to be discovered about the mind and its connections to the world.

The human brain may very well have powers we don't understand!

Is ESP Real?

So what's the bottom line? Is ESP real or not? Scientists can't say for sure. But stories of people who claim to know the future, read others' thoughts, or "see" things using only the mind have fascinated humans for centuries. If you're interested in parapsychology, maybe someday you'll be the one to prove whether or not ESP exists!

Believe It or Not!

- Samuel Clemens, better known as Mark Twain, was born in 1835, a year when Halley's comet orbited Earth. The comet passes Earth every seventy-five years. Long before his death, Clemens said he came into the world on the tail of the comet and he'd leave on the comet's tail too. And that's just what he did. Clemens died in 1910, as the comet returned. ESP or coincidence?

- Some people report feeling as if they've already experienced an event that's currently happening. This is called déjà vu and is often considered a form of ESP.

- Sonya Fitzpatrick was diagnosed with severe hearing loss as a child. Yet she claimed she could hear and talk to animals on their farm. These days she is one of the world's most famous animal communicators, appearing on TV, writing books, and working with pets to help them overcome fears.

Glossary

clairvoyance: using the mind to see another place or event

coincidence: events that happen by chance

evidence: facts that prove whether something is true or not

friction: the resistance one surface creates when moving over another

hoax: a scheme or made-up story

paranormal: beyond normal scientific understanding

parapsychology: the study of paranormal or psychic abilities

precognition: knowing something will happen before it does

prophecy: a prediction

séance: a meeting led by a medium who tries to communicate with the dead

telekinesis: the mental ability to move or control objects

telepathy: mind reading or communicating thoughts with just the mind

Learn More about ESP

Books

Olson, Elsie. *Are You Psychic? Facts, Trivia, and Quizzes*. Minneapolis: Lerner Publications, 2018. Learn more about ESP, premonitions, and whether some people are really able to see into the future—and discover whether *you* may have a sixth sense!

Owings, Lisa. *ESP*. Minneapolis: Bellwether Media, 2015. Owings takes a fun, close-up look at ESP.

Perish, Patrick. *Is ESP Real?* Mankato, MN: Amicus, 2014. Do more research into whether ESP is true or just a hoax.

Websites

How Stuff Works: "What Is Déjà Vu?"
http://science.howstuffworks.com/science-vs-myth/extrasensory-perceptions/question657.htm
Explore the topic of déjà vu at this interesting site.

Thought Co.: "6 Signs That You Might Be Psychic"
https://www.thoughtco.com/signs-you-might-be-psychic-2594880
Check out this list of signs that you might have a sixth sense.

Index

Photo Acknowledgments

The images in this book are used with the permission of: © iStockphoto.com/allanswart, p. 4; © Bowie15/Dreamstime.com, p. 5; © iStockphoto.com/ljubaphoto, p. 6; Everett Historical/Shutterstock.com, p. 7; © Stockyimages/Dreamstime.com, p. 8; © iStockphoto.com/3quarks, p. 9; Photographee.eu/Shutterstock.com, p. 10; AP Photo/Mark Lennihan, p. 11; Giannis Katsaros/Alamy Stock Photo, p. 12; INTERFOTO/Alamy Stock Photo, p. 13; Martin Shields/Alamy Stock Photo, p. 14; Everett Collection Historical/Alamy Stock Photo, p. 15; Chronicle/Alamy Stock Photo, pp. 16, 23; © iStockphoto.com/VikramRaghuvanshi, p. 17; © Vladm/Dreamstime.com, p. 18; REUTERS/Alamy Stock Photo, p. 19; Simon Stanford/Alamy Stock Photo, p. 20; AP Photo/Stephen Trupp/STAR MAX/IPx, p. 21; AP Photo/Bob Jordan, p. 22; © Milkovasa/Dreamstime.com, p. 24; AP Photo/Terry Renna, p. 25; © EVA HAMBACH/AFP/Getty Images, p. 26; © iStockphoto.com/fotografixx, p. 27; © iStockphoto.com/Zhenikeyev, p. 28.

Cover: © iStockphoto.com/iLexx.

Main body text set in Adrianna Regular 14/20.
Typeface provided by Chank.